Layering The Fig Tree

and

Other Family Feelings

by

Claire Gathercole

First published in 2006 by Wisteria Cottage Publishing Ltd.

ISBN: 9798357924483

PublishNation
www.publishnation.co.uk

These poems are dedicated to all the members
of my family both past and present whose love
has inspired them, and especially to Doris London,
my mother, who first gave me my love of words.

Writing with much care
we create another world
to contain our words.

CONTENTS

Imagine

Reflections

Ramblings

Voices

Feelings

Cooking It

Stories

Blessings

Imagine

What's in a head

She takes her head off to examine it
relieved to find two eyes that work
a nose, two ears, a mouth
all in passable shape
no problems yet.

Her skin's another matter.
It begins to blotch and pock
with a brown that soon defeats
attempts to cover it while
wrinkles riot.

She turns it upside down to see the dreams.
Ay, there's the rub. She pokes and prods
to see if memory is still intact,
if words still mean what
she intends to say.

She pops the pills in one by
two by three. This will increase
the flow of blood into the brain,
that should prevent dementia
her ardent hope.

Her head replaced she rings
her friend and laughs
at her funny ways, sits back on her
chair in her Monday face
ready for work.

White Geese

It is the honk
that sends me out
to watch the clouds.
Did I imagine it
or was it real?

I strain my eyes
against the sun
and then I see
them lustrous as
rare pearls in the clear sky

They swirl and call
and beat their wings
to speed them on
as they take turns
to head their ragged V

and face what comes.
No priceless swans
are here but with
this company of geese
I can now fly …

Take Wing

Take up your grief or joy and find
an enigmatic voice to search it out
and beat it with an irony of mind.
Then use an allegory to explore
the boundaries of your thought.

You could take wing upon a metaphor
soaring high up in the heavens blue above,
or digging deep to open up your head
shower ashes on it, to damp down
the fires that threaten to ignite the whole.

Then roar your voice across the seas
until the hills take up your cry
and tumble down the lava from their souls
forcing to flee tormentors old and new
to vanish in the mistiness of time ago.

But do not use sarcasm born of fear
the mockers mockery cast out should be
to allow a human voice to laugh and love
a human heart to see.

An imaginative lad

He stands and thinks and watches,
holding back not wanting to be seen.
A silent boy
who yet can make a noise as loud as any.

Gentle hands he has,
creative as he builds or draws with care.
He tries to be a clown to make us laugh
but like the clown, he's sensitive, soon sad.
An imaginative lad.

He has an awkward streak
at times unsatisfied and obstinate
but yet a kindness there
that's rare -
a child to make you glad.

A Sacred Map

As I mapped his face with my fingers
the dream was broken.
As I mapped his eyes with my gaze
the un-knowing in the bright light
became springs of pure water.
As I mapped the bones of his fingers and toes
the magnetism of the north was there –

So this was the origin, I thought.
This was the origin of the adult map
that was to come.

A Symphony of Swans

A gleam of white flying low
inspires me, especially
when in twos or threes
together they
spread their wings
and take off.

"But they've become a nuisance,"
says the ferryman

"Why spread their wings and fly
outrageously, when they can swim?
They've all they need upon
the river. They do not
need to flap about
and hoot
disturbing people.

"Yes, they've become a nuisance,"
says the ferryman.

"And they can dive to feed
or make a nest among the reeds
to mate and rear
their young. This
should be all they need.
Why worry more
and try to soar?"

"But ferryman I have to try to fly.
You surely do not need to ask the reason why."

Reflections

Reflections

Who can reflect the colours of the mind?
The deep dark midnight blue lit
by a silver moon to shadow-scare.

The torn grey-green of early morning light
hazed soft-etched pearl-glazed mist
lifting to reveal its sun-lit promise.

Scarlet-faced energy turned to russet now
by ochre mix of school-girl brown and gold
that glistens to reveal a childish face.

We have no need of coal-dust hard-faced black
to shake its miseries upon us all and
cover clarity beneath its beastly weeping feet.

The prunus lends us sunlit sparkle flowers
while candlelight reflects in endless hovering white
the sparking of the flame that holds our gaze.

Eclipse   11.11 am August 11th 1999

Why do we embrace
the mystery of it all.
The hush of evening
at midday,
the darkness fall,
the sun a nibbled cheese
glowing behind the wispy clouds,
the dusk-like chill?

We hold our breath
till all our senses fill
with a burning yearning,
heightened by the fiery glow
that though reduced still
dominates with a ring
of promise,
a crown of light...

and with all our skill and might
we fail and fade without it.

The Gathering

Because they had seen the signs
or heard it spoken of
or read the words
they began to gather.

Some walked the path together
close in deep communication,
while others drove the beasts of burden
that they loved the most
or flew with wings or pedals
to get there in time.

Imagine what it was like as they arrived!
Eye lit to eye as they
beheld the signs and sounds that
beckoned them.
Heart leapt to heart as the
throaty music drove deep
into their souls.

It was a gathering
to drive the world and all its
cares away for some short time,
and they began to glimpse
those higher things long
hidden from their eyes
and long desired.

Eventide

The colours of the dusk
elude us now..
that hushed luminous
magenta of the eventide
that lulls us into stillness
as our eyes become
accustomed to the
deepening violet shadows,
the tracery of a branch
against the darkening
sky, the glisten
of a puddle, the flitting
of a bat, while
our ears strain to hear
the soft mellow
hooting of an owl.

Our senses tell us
this is the time to think
this is the time
to pray, to meditate
in silence on the day
or go rambling
with the one we love,
voicing in the quiet
all our hopes and fears.

No loud voice or music here,
no bright light.

The soft coverlet of
velvet blackness is all we need
as we wait for the distant
twinkle of the evening star
to lead us
through the night.

Waiting

When I have seen how every day we wait
and waiting soon becomes a way of life,
stretched from our hopeful youth until this date
and all that happens simply twists the knife.

When I have seen how age brings on decay
and there is nothing that can halt the pull
to bring us down to naught without delay
and empty out all that was once so full.

When I have seen how love can wait in vain
still looking forward to a time of peace
while grief and fear have made it all too plain
there's nothing here that will extend our lease.

Waiting has taught me to enjoy today,
tomorrow may not ever come my way.

A hard time she had of it

"Where are those Wise Men then!"
"Please Miss, two of them are stuck in the floods."
And so the solitary king came into view
solemn as an eight-year-old girl.

But what if there had only been one
having a cold coming of it?
And what if she was a wise woman
led by her intuition to find the star?

What then would her gift have been?

Would a woman offer gold
knowing kingship needs no recognition?

Perhaps the beguiling perfumed frankincense
would have seemed most important
loving as she does to waft the scent of peace
between God and humankind?

But what of the myrrh?
Would she have carried that carefully with her fears
knowing herself no stranger to the grief of a death
foreshadowed in a birth?

A hard time she had of it
washing his feet with her tears
anointing him for death.

*Reflecting on a school Nativity Play when there
really was only one Wise 'Man' and she was a
little girl!*

15

Dancing Feet

The music was romping
in my head
and would not be put down,
but flowed out into my fingers
and my toes
demanding action.
I banged the keys
to find the tune
and stroked them
until the melody sang
clear and strong.
Then my feet left the pedals
and began to beat the time
and leap high and higher
compelled to express
all my dreams in the dance
and marvel that it was at once
an affirmation and an offering.

Ramblings

Town Brook Hollow

Was it the soft-slipped rain
upon their faces that
drove them on?
now from hill to vale
Or the challenge
of those other walks
when children ran ahead
or dragged behind and
all seemed fresh and new
a wilderness of wonder
to explore.

Did the soft-bosoms
of the hills promise that
they could lift up
their eyes for help?

They meant simply to stroll
and stray along the walk
they knew so well,
but once embarked upon it
they could not stop.
The rain that could have been
their excuse
instead encouraged them
and made them laugh,
their struggle with the elements
somehow confirming their wish
to stay on course and battle on.

And then the sun came out…
Now it was tears
that wet their cheeks
as gorse gleamed golden
while bracken softened
it with rusty brown
and heathers' muted pink
glimpsed here and there,
bright water burbling in
its timeless course …

Such beauty took their
breath away
with rainbows skipping
to make them
gasp at such wild
abandoned
colourful
profusion,
daring them
to give up
In face of
such a joy.

18

The Visit

I remembered her
young,
pretty,
dark,
fragile,
walking with two sticks,
laughing.
She now bears
constant 10-years-old pain,
double vision,
nausea,
a catheter,
a hoist to get her to the loo,
her bowels carefully organised to evacuate to plan,
patronising people,
dilatory doctoring,
crucifying christians.
She spoke with humour of her stroke
and six-week stay in hospital, framed
around consultants' holidays,
while she languished helpless
in soaring,
fearful,
uncontrollable pain.
She's better now, but worse.
She has lost more.
Her hand won't work.
There never was a remedy.
All she can do now is play
with ideas in her head.

Car Journey

Here we are folded into the car together.
I relax, let out a sigh of contentment.
It's a three hour journey,
we cannot be interrupted.
We are cloistered here
for now in silent harmony
feeling each others presence
as all that we hold dear.

There is no need of words to begin with.
Our individual thoughts roam freely
until they bubble up
and spill out in the odd word.
We point out this or that,
we laugh or sigh
and our minds feel their way
into each other's orbit.

With eyes ahead upon the road our mind
is strangely concentrated and free
of most distractions.
And sometimes thought
can be expressed in a deeper way
as we explore ideas and questions
that time and circumstance usually forbid
us to dwell upon or say.

But wait there is an intruder here again
to shatter our peace and our discussions
that brings the outside word
into our space and quiet
with its raucous insistent tone.
Let us not to the marriage of
true minds admit impediment.
Switch off the mobile phone!

Siesta

No gardening today.
It is too hot
and so I sit and
contemplate.
The dove is cooing
- that summer sound
of sleepiness.
The soft breeze begins
to stir the drooping leaves
with the promise of some
cooler air,
while the honey bee
swings on the lavender
as he sips the nectar
in an English garden.

My grandchildren are playing
on some faraway beach in Portugal
where the heat is shimmering
in ever more intense waves
forcing them to find the water
or some shade for a siesta.

I wonder if their parents remember
that wet Welsh summer when
we were forced to stay in all day
or walk out in the rain –
and chose the latter.

Or do they remember that
crazy French parrot in Sanary
who would 'sing' a bar or two of
La Marseillaise and end off key
making us laugh during our
siesta there,
while our daughter
shed a tear for her
boyfriend back at home.

Siesta,
a hot and dreamy time…

Voices

Don't touch

Don't touch! don't touch!

So they didn't touch
but passed on by
leaving a boy of ten
to bleed and die.

If I cry ...

If I cry Dad will sigh,
he will ask the reason why.
My brothers will be cross,
that's their loss,
they always get their way,
never let me play.
But Mum's in a hurry,
she'll worry.
She'll say,
"Now then you three,
it's very nearly time for tea."
Then she'll give me a hug
and fill up my mug
FIRST!

Down Time

"The shed still gloomily
unfinished . . .
Feels like what we need
is more **down** time!"

Ah yes, down time –
that moment of release
when I can please myself

that space to be alone
and muse
and ponder deep
of better things ..

I need down time
when I am in
the midst of things
not as a far-off hope
when things ease up
or I retire…

The forgotten words

"It's difficult to talk now,"
she said,
"because I can't remember
the words…

"What is happening
about ….
and how is it that
they are going
to …

"Oh, who?"

"You know …
You know who
I mean …
I mean them..
Yes, them.
They've been away
they say
I want to go there
to stay..
to stay
there ..
there with them.
It was tough
you know ..

"Oh what was
tough .." ?

"Oh yes, the meat
was tough..
It made it difficult
to see where
they were …
"I cannot
get my head straight."

Women's Words

'Help, help' …
I need your words
to crystallise
into memories
that stay upon the page

'Help, help' …
my stomach
still curdles
when I recall
her hopeless cry

'Help, help' …
she was a women
of many words
until dementia
took them all away

'Help, help' …
she would utter
in a thin reedy voice
as she slithered
to the floor.

'Help, help'…
those family stories
that I need
to understand
were in her head.

'Help, help' …
now I struggle on
to write things down
before it is
too late
and the shadow reaches me …

She is Mute

She uses her ears
pricking them up
to make sure she
hears and understands
what is happening
around her.

She uses her nose,
pressing it wet and warm
onto any flesh
she can find that
will not shrink away.

She uses her eyes
eloquently as they
plead with you to
join her game
or to give her love.

She uses her paw
prodding selectively
now and then
to make her point.

She uses her bark
and a low growl
when she is
alarmed
or yet afraid.

She is, of course, a dog –
the one mute in a
family of vocal children.

What would she give
to find her voice
and join the conversation!

Words of Love

"To dear little ..."
my mother-in-law
would write
on her presents.

"With much love"
I write on mine –
my only outlet
for those words of love
bottled up inside.
which cannot be spoken
without embarrassment
and spill out
when we address
our Christmas gifts instead.

So love is passed
up and down the family
in decorated parcels
like small prayers
with carefully worded
messages which we
unwrap with care
and roll up in our minds.

Feelings

Best to let the sunshine in

It is a sunshine day
        and so I look for golden words
to embark with, weaving
        in and out of the
beams of liquid light
        which flow so freely
and bring us warmth
        in this place of space –

Let the heat
        expand into those
molten drops that walk
        on the water of our minds
and fill our pages with the murmur
        of their expectations,
while liquid light and shade
        lend deep shadows to our thought.

Here where the lofty pillars lift our eyes
        to the extended view,
the octagonal symmetry stretches out to us
        bending our narrow perspective
to shift and discover anew
        how best to let the sunshine in
and catch the mooring ropes
        that ring this place.

Her father's daughter

I let you down so badly that I wince
Each time I think of it. A daughter
Should be the light behind your eye
To cheer the aches and pains
That come with age and carry all
Your troubles with her own.
She has a role to smooth
The wrinkles on your brow
To calm your cares.

But nowadays she lives too far away
And she can only visit for a day.

Stumble-slow

Have you seen him walking stumble-slow, eyes low?
His bones ache and his breath strains heavily
as he forces one frail leg in front of another
his frame spare and emaciated from age.

They watch. He doesn't see them now -
No longer raises his hat and smiles and stops
to pass the time of day with caring chat
and gentle smile that leaves them happy.

Instead they stare after him and shudder as
they see him falter and clutch the fence again.
Is he in pain? Or does the effort of living
take so dear a toll and leave a skeleton

that slowly empties of all that they
once knew and treasured as a man of worth,
generous and loving. His gifts he'll share again
they know as he moves on and leaves his shell

behind to find his wings and fly.

Roll along, role along

Roll along, roll along, roll along with me ..

There once was a woman whose roles
she kept at far different poles
as she found if she tried
to combine and confide
that all she could do was a roll.

Ah all those roles to play -
which will it be today
who can say?

A housewife to keep the house clean,
a mother she surely has been,
a wife who was always just there,
a gardener who had quite a flair,
a daughter to take the rebuke,
a Nana, a wonderful fluke.

Roll along, roll along, roll along with me ..

But what of a yet other role,
which hasn't yet taken its toll -
will she find if she tries,
and still deeper she sighs,
that she will end up on a roll.

Ah all those roles to play -
which will it be today
who can say?

A friend who can still give a shout,
a helper to those who're in doubt,
a visitor to those in need,
a listener to those we should heed,
a reader whose interest is sure,
a traveller to take on a tour,
a believer in all we hold dear,
an encourager never fear.

Roll along, roll along, roll along with me ...

Dread

I've got it again, Lord,
it is such a pain,
that feeling of dread
that's attacking my brain.

The event that I fear
is ages ahead.
I cannot control it
or put it to bed.

I'm afraid that I'll fail
to get there on time,
that I'll choke on the food
or spill their good wine.

That my loved ones will suffer
in some awful smash,
that my car will break down
and the stock market crash!

I'm praying so hard, Lord,
my heart is like lead.
Take care of those times
that I look on with dread!

Late Wasp Limerick

I was stung by a wasp that was late
He was really beginning to hate
Humans who tried
To wave him outside
And seal his already sad fate.

Visiting Old Friends

It was so nice of you to let us stay
and talk with you. It did us so much good.
It seems a long time since we went away.

You haven't changed at all in any way -
you still delight us in that way you could.
It was so nice of you to let us stay

Life charges on, we struggle in the fray
to work hard and do all we think we should.
It seems a long time since we went away

We're older now, there is no time to play
at life and love. We must do what we would.
It was so nice of you to let us stay.

Life's tempo makes it harder to repay
your kindness dear, so does our parenthood.
It seems a long time since we went away

Old friends like you renew our hope today
that some are still so kind and still so good.
It was so nice of you to let us stay,
it seems a long time since we went away.

Cooking It

The Honey Pot

Honey, honey,
I taste it on my tongue
in hot French markets.
I buy
a jar here a tub there
as a memento of our visit
to eat on cold grey days
in England,
to remind me ..
j'y pense.

Honey, honey,
I look for great big tubs of it to feed
the grandson who loves it best
plus one or more for each family
to be used as needed
to tranquillise
et être tout miel.

Honey, honey,
I remember how
he used to call
me 'Honey' in
those early days
when our eyes
would liquefy and melt
into each other ..
'mielleux'.

Honey, "Honey
makes the love
taste sweeter,"
writes Isobel
on our fridge door.
Even at nine-years-old
she begins to understand
the need for that
'douceur'.

Honey, honey,
"Un grand pot, s'il vous plait"
to spread around ...

Blackberrying

Brambles tearing,
scratching at legs and hands.
Clothing caught. The luscious,
shiny, vitamin-filled black fruit picked
then dropped,
plopped
alas into the briars.
Another sun-kisses the mouth
with desire for more.
Back warmth,
stretching and reaching,
for the best are always high
on a wild runner
soaring over the rambling mound of prickles.
The purple-stained fingers,
seeds under the nails,
pick the fruit carefully for bramble jelly,
blackberry and apple pie.
The bag on wrist swells
and sways and fills the senses
with our success.
The fragrant air tickles the nostrils
with the appetite of autumn.

Jam Making

Browsing the hedgerows
for ripe blackberries,
searching for rose hips
and for crab apples,
watching our mothers
boil up delicious jam.
Hurrying home from school to eat
quince jelly as a tea-time treat.

Running now with life
at such a pace our children are
trying to counteract the sour taste
of time's destruction in a different way.
Blue-ing their tongues and fingers
with their instruments
leading our imaginations on,
stimulating our souls
with their inventive jazz trumpet.

Jamming the smell,
the flavour, the sugar -
stirring, stirring the sound
into the blue, red fruit,
dripping it slowly through muslin bags,
the whole night long –
testing, testing
the jam temperature
dripping the jazz slowly
into warmed pots of liquid sound
to taste and to enjoy.

Reinventing the world
as it fills our minds.

Treacle Tart

I send each child a
book of recipes:

Use your fingers
to crumble breadcrumbs
and rub the fat into the flour
then add the water
- not too much.
Roll out the pastry lovingly,
- if it's too brittle it will break
too thick is stodgy and so hard to eat .

Put in a tin
the crumbs on top of it,
with large spoonfuls
of golden syrup dribbled in
- no, not too much or it will cloy
and you'll soon tire of it,
too little and it's like cardboard
in your mouth.

The cook deserves to lick the spoon
while it is cooking in the oven,
but don't forget to watch it
does not burn
and take away the flavour
that you love.

Now serve it up
- a slice for everyone.
Yes, eat with fingers
then it tastes the best
and stickiness is
something to be shared.

Stories

Layering the Fig Tree

And I remember
how in the late evening
of his life
my father grew
fig trees in his garden.
Their leaves large and glossy
in the summer sun
provided shade and refreshment
for his visitors.

"They are delicious,"
he would say
plucking a fig and pressing
it into my hand.
"Do try it. I'm sure
you will enjoy the flavour
as it bursts into your mouth."

I didn't like the slimy seeds
upon my tongue,
but with eager eyes upon me
it was hard to disappoint
and tell him so.

Nor could we say 'No'
when he started to
bend the branches
and tie them down,
layering them to give us
small fig trees in pots
for us to grow

---ooo000ooo---

I now layer fig trees
for my offspring too.
It seems they're
always dying
and must be replaced.

And the fruit so seldom
ripens in this colder clime.

The Posy Ring

I was a child
when my mother taught me
how to pick flowers
and arrange them
in her posy ring.

That posy ring
now sits upon my shelf
and I search my garden
for her flowers.

The weeping willow
will no longer serve,
but winter jasmine
gives me golden stars
and honeysuckle still
struggles to produce
its lace of gold and white
to scent the air.
Penstemon freely
curves its drops
of ruby red
towards the earth,
while lavender
and rosemary
add fragrance
to my quest ..

to continue
the theme
she left to me.

The Stranger's Map

How do we map ourselves
far, far from home
in this strange place?
Why are we here
and who are we?

Our identity is bound up
in family and friends.
We map each other
and we know them all
as they know us.

The map we follow here
is not our map. It does
not lead us to the folk
we know and love.
We cannot read it well.

This is a map we have not
learned. We do not
understand what it is telling us
about ourselves. We cannot
find where we belong …

For we are strangers here
and long for home.

The Two Grandmothers

I often wondered about the very large pores
on her nose, which she was always powdering.
Pat. Pat. Pat.

"Have you brought me any ice-cream?"
She would ask my mother.

I loved ice-cream too, but I wasn't offered any
and we would sit and watch my grandmother eat.

It was my other grandmother's ears which
fascinated me most. They had holes in them .. not
that she wore any earrings these days as they would
have fallen out.

"Let that be a warning to you," my Mother would
say. "She's too vain, always dolling herself up.
Mutton dressed up as lamb."

This was not the only awful advice I was given
about my father's mother. She'd always have
something spilled down her front. What's more
she liked winkles and was brazen enough to go
and buy some from those stalls down by the station
where 'nice' people didn't go.

"She uses her hair pins to eat them with too,"
said my mother.

I was fascinated. Perhaps that was why her hair
grips were so different from mine which were strong
and straight and held my hair in place, while hers
were wiggly and curly and seemed to have no useful function –
apart from the winkles, I suppose.

Drowning

It was the eye contact, however brief, which made me realise that the situation was desperate.

Borne on a flood tide of people, I was fighting to survive, struggling against all the odds to reach the shore in a quiet haven where my journey could be completed in peace. The time was late, the tide would not wait for me, those who expected me would examine every minute of delay and exclaim over it, the worry creasing their elderly brows. How could I fail them?

How could I fail her as the blows flayed down on her and she was sinking, sinking down, soon to be out of sight as the tide flowed over her?

I didn't fail them. I fought my way through the crowds and caught the train with hardly a moment to spare. I sank down with relief to complete my journey, sinking, sinking down as my mind tried to obliterate the sight of her and to pretend I had not seen her, it had not happened.

There had been no cry that I had heard. My ears were full of the noise of the tube trains and the feet of the people, running, running. No talking, no laughing. Intent faces, eyes fixed like mine, determined not to see her plight or go to her aid. An arm to lift her or defend her from a blow, a cry of help, however strangled, might have penetrated the rush hour panic and stemmed the tide so that she could be helped.

I was not the only one who did not help. But I had read the Good Samaritan. I knew the score.

Navigating towards dawn

The mist closes in so quickly
on us here
and the rain squalls down
obliterating
the sound of the strident sea,
whose foam-ridged waves
I loved to surf
but which now menace me
with a stern power
I would still like to tame
but dare not try.

The dawn is coming in at 4 am
and how I long for it,
watching, waiting for those
first golden streaks of light
telling my pain-laden passenger
there is not long now
before the firey match
ignites the burning beacon
and brings its hope to stay.

Those hard-eyed faces
press down on me
offering me no escape
from my predicament
as my jelly-filled legs
stumble in the vicious surf
and I fall down.
I cannot face them out
wrecked as I am
and overwhelmed –
until the shining angel wing
lights my gaze and holds it
so that I sleep a short breathless while.

I navigate in and out
of the pain that haunts me
perplexed and powerless,
treading the waves with
shaky, zigzag steps,
fending off the battering
they give with any small relief
that comes to hand –
distractions all, that search
for a break that will allow
me to dream again.

Blessings

I would bring you ...

I would bring you wonder –
   the wonder of a bay
   white sand skirted deep azure blue
   mysterious mountains still in view.

I would bring you hope –
   the hope that comes from knowledge
   of the love that understands
   and brings peace in its hands.

I would bring you happiness –
   the happiness of being
   with those whose love and laughter
   make a fresh way of seeing.

I would bring you tenderness –
   the tender love which finds a way
   through the pain, no need to say
   a word or shed a tear..

I will pray for you ...

A Blessing

May you be blessed with laughter
in your soul
May you know wonder and delight
in simple things
May you make music
in your heart
May you play with words
in your head
May you create much beauty
with your hands
May you be a seeker
after truth

May you understand the needs of others
and respond
May you hear the cry of the desolate
and weep
May you know your own shortcomings
and grieve
May you be saved from the corrosion
of despair

May you walk with love and joy
throughout your life

May the peace of the Lord be with you
always.

Who Am I?

I AM IN MY MOTHER'S TEAR
I AM IN MY FATHER'S WINK
I AM IN MY HUSBAND'S EYE
I AM IN MY DAUGHTER'S THOUGHT
I AM IN MY SON'S CONSCIENCE
I AM IN MY GRANDSONS' HOPES
I AM IN GRANDDAUGHTERS' DREAMS
I HOLD THE BABY IN MY ARMS.

MY MOTHER'S IN HER DAUGHTER'S HEAD
MY FATHER'S IN HIS DAUGHTER'S SOUL
MY HUSBAND'S IN HIS WIFE'S LONGING
MY DAUGHTER'S IN HER MOTHER'S CARE
MY SON IS IN HIS MOTHER'S SMILE
GRANDSONS ARE IN THEIR GRANDMA'S PRIDE
GRANDDAUGHTERS ARE GRANDMA'S DELIGHT
THE BABY'S IN OUR HOPES AND PRAYERS

I AM MYSELF HOW I CAN SEE
MY OFFSPRING ARE BOUND UP IN ME

Printed in Great Britain
by Amazon